Dad's Pizza

Daniel Levine
Illustrated by Chantal Stewart

My dad loves to make pizza.

"We could open a pizza restaurant!" he says.

"We would need lots of flour," Mom says.

"We would need lots of sauce," Mitzi says.

"We would need lots of cheese," I say.

"We would need lots of toppings," Mom says.

"We would need lots of plates," Mitzi says.

"We would need lots of people to wash dishes," I say.

"I think I'll make pizza just for us!" Dad says.
"Let's eat!"